On Top Of The World And Down In The Depths

My unexpected adventure deep in the highest mountains of India

W. A. Schofield

DEDICATION

To all Tibetans who live inside and outside of Tibet.

CONTENTS

ACKNOWLEDGMENTS

Special thanks to friend and colleague, Elizabeth Kutter Ph.D., biology faculty member emerita at The Evergreen State College, who supported the writing of this story every step of the way, including right down to the final edit. Thanks to my initial editor, Keith Eisner, who offered excellent suggestions and much encouragement through several early drafts. Thanks also to dear friends Julie Rodwell and Margo Westfall, who kindly read this story, made excellent suggestions and occasionally asked for more details.

1 A TRIP OF A LIFETIME

One day, in 1986, a question pops out of the blue that changes my life. "Would you like to read a book about an ancient culture of Buddhists who live near Tibet?" asks my friend Bebe — a tall, slender blond in her 50's.

"Indeed I would," say I — a short, less slender blond in my 40's.

'A Journey in Ladakh' was written by Andrew Harvey, a Shakespearian scholar at Oxford University. In lyrical language, Harvey describes his arduous and spiritual adventure to the highest part of India, where Buddhists have meditated since three centuries before Christ and still practice a pure form of Buddhism today. Harvey writes about the culture, customs and Buddhist ideals of people who live in Ladakh as being similar to the styles of Tibetans, who live nearby. This region is called 'Little Tibet'.

Fascinated by Harvey's story, Bebe and I imagine taking a trip to Ladakh in three years. By then Bebe's youngest child will be 18 and my three children will have flown the coop, at which point we could consider a 'high adventure' of this nature. Going to Ladakh could give Bebe a break from her crumbling marriage and an opportunity to explore alternatives. Ladakh would offer me a change from raising three children as a single mother, and a chance for a new perspective on life.

Surrounded by the spectacular Himalayan Mountains, Ladakh,

7,000 miles from America, is some twelve to sixteen thousand feet above sea level. Ladakh is the closest to Tibet that we can go since China, after invading Tibet in 1950, closed Tibet's borders to visitors. Bebe and I make the mammoth decision to take the trip of a lifetime. Our children ask WHY? They think we are crazy to enter a remote region, so far away! We explain that our reason for going springs from our ignited imagination after reading about an ancient culture of Buddhists who still live there today. They know nothing of what we speak. We assure them that all possible precautions will be taken.

Over the next three years, Bebe and I make our plans. We figure we will need 2,500 dollars each to cover airfare, food, and accommodations for a three-week stay. We pour over maps of the region and pencil in routes. We each lay out our backpacks, sleeping bag, walking boots, flashlight, water bottles, dried nuts and fruit, camp stove, and clothes for heat and cold. We include a first aid kit — with pills to stop diarrhea. We buy notepaper, pens, and an old movie camera to record our 'Journey in Ladakh.' With minimal travel experience, heavy backpacks and high enthusiasm, Bebe and I leave Seattle for the Far East in August 1988.

After a nine-hour jumbo jet flight from Washington State we land in Tokyo and wait six hours at the airport to change planes. The next jet flies for eight hours to land us mid-summer in hot and steamy Delhi, with twenty-four hours to spend before our flight to Ladakh. We take a taxi to a busy part of Delhi where the sights, sounds and smells on the streets send my mind in a whirl. Horns from buses and cars blare, motorbikes rev, bicycle bells ring, and drivers of carts drawn by oxen, horse or a donkey scream for a clear trail through the mass of confusion. Cows, considered holy in India, amble freely along the narrow streets. Offsetting the olfactory offenses of cow, horse and donkey dung that litter the road and the occasional whiff of a person taking relief in a gutter are the aromas of jasmine, lotus flowers and the pungent spices of cardamom, cinnamon, coriander, and cumin, to name a few of India's many spices for sale by the road.

A family of four rides by on a scooter. A toddler precariously perches on the handlebar in front of her father, while the mother holds tightly to her husband's waist; her veil trails in the wind past a teenage boy on the back of the scooter, who grips her shoulders. Some women walk by, adorned in colorful veils and saris. Men in white dhotis — a rectangular piece of cloth wrapped around their middle and legs — knotted at the waist. It resembles a long skirt. Some men wear a western style suit and tie. Few women appear to have changed their dress code.

Thin men, women, and children — barefoot, in rags, with big brown eyes set in hollow cheeks — beg for something — anything. An emaciated old man in a dirty white dhoti, a long beard, and straggly hair staggers by, using an old tree limb to prop up his body. Bone-thin dogs search every nook and cranny for food.

In need of reprieve from seeing such suffering, Bebe and I enter a roadside café for a cup of tea. A small, slim Indian man wearing a smart Western suit stops by our table. He says, "May I sit with you?" Bebe replies, "Yes you may." I don't mind. He seems harmless enough. This small dark man stares at tall fair Bebe with saucer-sized eyes. She returns his gaze. Her light blue eyes drop to a soft, 'doe-like' Lauren Bacall expression. I watch him melt.

After our answering pleasantries concerning where we are from and what brings us to India, he says, "I manufacture silk and sell it all over the world." We are impressed. I say, "May we see silkworms in action, and the harvesting and weaving of silk?" Mr. Silk-man says, "Unfortunately, given the twenty-four hours you are in Delhi, my factory is too far away. However, in my apartment, I can show you the finest silk ever made."

Hmm! Wooed by silk, I wonder if we will be safe. But there are two of us and he is smaller than either of us. We agree to go. Mr. Silk-man hails a taxi and off we ride through the back streets of Delhi, to where we don't know. Eventually, we stop at a pleasant-looking three-story apartment building, located amidst a block of similarly shaped buildings of different colors. In a pink one, we climb three flights of stairs to Mr. Silk-man's space, which consists of a small living room, a kitchen, a bathroom and two bedrooms. It is clean and comfortable, with reams of silk of every color hanging all about.

Despite Mr. Silk-man's obvious attraction to Bebe, he includes me in the conversation. We sit in cushy cushions to chat over tea and sweet cakes. He goes to his bedroom and comes out with his prize — a long, wide piece of the finest cream-colored silk I have ever seen. So light in weight and fine in texture, I can barely feel it, as if an eiderdown goose feather floats by. Mr. Silk-man gathers the gossamer cloth into a tiny ball in the palm of his hand. When he opens his palm, I watch the silk spring to its original size — in awe at the miracle of worm threads.

Coming down to earth, I remind Bebe that we still need to find a place to stay. As we stand to leave, Mr. Silk-man says we are welcome to stay the night. "Sure," says Bebe enthusiastically. "Where will we sleep?" I ask anxiously. He points to the 'other' bedroom, with twin beds. "Okay," I say, feeling uneasy.

Mr. Silk-man takes us out to a fancy Indian restaurant where he proudly introduces his fair Western women to the owner, who greets us reverently. Sitar and tabla musicians play in the corner as the aroma of incense and spices floats in the air. Tables, covered with starched white linen, are set with napkins placed around a bowl of intoxicating jasmine flowers. Mr. Silk-man guides us to a discreet spot. We are offered iced water, lemonade or tea, wine or beer. Orange pekoe tea is for me.

For dinner, I begin with poppadoms: light crispy saucer-sized wafers made from split pea flour. I break the poppadoms into pieces and dip them in various chutneys. My favorite chutney is made from fresh mangos, ginger root, salt, sugar, white vinegar, raisins and garlic powder — with optional cayenne pepper. I choose the 'option.' The heat sets my mouth on fire — nothing to compare with the heat that emanates from Mr. Silk-man and Bebe across the table as the sitar and tabla music play on in a blissful circular pattern.

For the main course, I order curried vegetables with basmati rice and raita — a cooling mixture of cucumber, onion, cumin, and yogurt. Utterly delectable. More delicious orange pekoe tea fills my cup as I relax further into the moment of eating genuine Indian food and listening to authentic Indian music. As I order dessert, Bebe and Mr. Silk-man are well underway with a dessert of their own. For me, the topping on the evening is banana halva, made from bananas fried in butter, mashed with sugar and rose water served in a sherbet glass, topped with ground cardamom and sliced almonds.

Mr. Silk-man generously pays the bill and orders a taxi to his apartment. Bebe and I retire to the second bedroom. Perhaps I hear footsteps in the night. Come morning, we take off for Ladakh, leaving a moonstruck Mr. Silk-man to dream on.

As we board the rickety 12-seater propeller plane, I look at Bebe with concern. Will this old flyer take us safely to Ladakh? She stares wordlessly into the distance. Wobbly as it is, the plane lifts off without a hitch. I watch propellers whirl through dirt splattered windows, as we cruise in a sparkling blue sky above the majestic Himalayan mountains whose jagged, snow-covered peaks and deep dark valleys appear ominous below.

Wonder overrides anxiety as I succumb to fate.

2 A TWIST OF FATE

With 30 hours of travel time under my belt, I stagger down the plane's rickety steps into the 'reality' of my 'fantasy' journey. After a scary squeeze between mountain peaks to a bumpy airstrip, surrounded by tall white beauty, we land safely in Ladakh under a blazing sun in a cloudless sky that bakes the red/brown earth into stone.

The sudden change from sea level to 12,000 feet makes me light-headed. In my oxygen-depleted state of confusion, I imagine we have landed on the moon. With heavy backpacks slung in place, Bebe and I walk the dusty mile to Leh, the central town in Ladakh. Prayer flags flutter in the wind along mountain passes, around temples and over houses. Streets of the red compressed earth in Leh are all a-bustle with the walk and talk of people. Chickens squawk, flutter, and peck about while yaks, goats, and sheep are herded through to be fed or to go to market. In tiny red bricked shops merchants sell barley bread, fruit, vegetables, pots and pans, bottled water, toilet paper and kerosene for stoves and lamps. The people of Leh greet us warmly in a singsong way. "Jullah! Jullah!" to which Bebe and I reply in unison, "Jullah. Jullah." We haven't a clue what it means until a Ladakhi man later tells us that "Jullah. Jullah" means "How are you, your mother and all?"

Most Ladakhi men and women are in the traditional attire called 'Goncha'. It is practical clothing for high altitude — a full length pleated brown robe made from homespun wool. Married women wear a colorful apron over it.

A man in his Goncha sports a five-inch tall, dark brown lamb's wool hat that turns up at the sides like the wings of a bird. His animal hide shoes curl up at the toe. Around her Goncha, a woman wears an embroidered waistband woven with geometric designs of red, blue, white, green and yellow. She sports knee-length brown felt boots. On her head, she wears a 'Perka' made of lamb's wool, embroidered with turquoise stones, that covers her head like a cobra's hood — tapering to a thin tail down her back.

I ask a tourist in hiking attire if she knows a good place to stay. She points to a small guesthouse up the hill and says, "The Falcon's Crest — run by a family — costs $5 a night."

Weary beyond measure, Bebe and I stagger up the hill, to be warmly greeted by a mother, father, and their teenage son. The parents say, "Jullah." The son says, "Yes, rooms ok?" Bebe and I choose separate rooms on the top floor, with a view of the barley fields all around and above the town of Leh. The only furniture in each room is a single wooden bed frame with a thin cotton mattress.

I lay my sleeping bag on top of the bed and lie down, happy to be horizontal, in anticipation — "to sleep perhaps to dream." No dreams for me. I lie awake all night, mercilessly attacked by bedbugs. These reddish-brown 'blood-suckers' the size of an apple seed hide during the day in the crevices of beds. They crawl out at night to find a warm body upon which to suck, which happens this night to be mine. Come daylight, red welts cover my body, which is apparently quite tasty. This is NOT part of my fantasy journey. Bebe's mattress is apparently bug-free. She sleeps soundly all night. The owners are apologetic and immediately replace my 'buggy' mattress with an equally thin 'fumigated' one. Despite the chemical odor, I sleep better from then on.

The shared toilet on the bottom floor is a hole in the ground, with no toilet paper. The smell of goats and chickens who live under the hotel permeates the air. Barley stored in the rafters helps sweeten it, along with the breeze sweeping in through the open windows from the fields and the mountains.

Meals at a small restaurant down the hill are simple and delicious, with local ingredients: barley, root vegetables, goat meat, milk, yogurt and cheese, chicken and eggs, apples and apricots. Common recipes use barley as a base for noodle soup and roasted barley flour kneaded for bread. A meal particular to Ladakh is a heavy pasta dish made from roasted barley flour and root vegetables. An omelet in the morning is a treat, although the egg yolks are almost white from not enough greens and bugs for chickens to eat.

Following advice from seasoned travelers before we left home, we eat only cooked food and drink hot tea or a mildly alcoholic drink brewed locally called chang — made from fermented barley — plus imported beer or bottled water. The downside of bottled water is evident in the many empty plastic bottles that litter this otherwise pristine environment. I resolve to become more 'mindful' of ways to avoid using plastic upon my return to America.

One day, while shopping in town for groceries, we meet Nawang, the Ladakhi man who told us the meaning of 'Jullah.' This handsome man, of medium height and build, wears Western-style jeans, shirt, and sneakers. He invites us to his home for tea. On the way, we see a string of prayer flags flying near the mighty Indus River. Nawang says that this river originates from the slopes of Mt. Kailash in Tibet and travels through Ladakh. It is 1,976 miles long, with tributaries that bring water downstream to millions of people in Asia.

We arrive at Nawang's modest abode, nestled in town, with prayer flags waving all around. Nawang tells us that prayer flags are a tradition in Tibet and Ladakh. They send good wishes in the wind to all people. The five colors are blue for sky, white for clouds, red for fire, green for water and yellow for earth. Ancient texts are printed on them like 'Om Mani Padme Hum' meaning, 'I salute the Jewel Within' — the 'Lotus Flower' symbolizing compassion — or 'The Mythical Wind Horse' — representing the speed of the wind with the strength of the horse.

Inside the tiny four-room house, we meet Nawang's parents, who bow, with hands in prayer, and say, "Jullah, Jullah." We return the gesture. They each wear a Goncha. The mother is about five feet tall and quite slender. She sports an apron over her Goncha to state that she is married. Her long jet-black hair, intertwined with pearls and turquoise beads, is braided and wrapped in circles around her head, like a crown. Nawang's father is slightly taller. He looks dignified in his simple attire. The mother shows Bebe and me around their house. The living room is cozy with images from ancient Tibet hanging on the walls. One sparsely furnished room, reserved for prayer, has a low table with lotus flowers painted on the surface, upon which rests a statue of Buddha. Small square carpets made of colored wool, woven into geometric designs are on the clean swept floor. We sit on the floor around the table and are offered 'Yak butter tea,' a traditional Ladakhi Tibetan drink made from Yak butter, salt, and hot water. It is ghastly. We drink it respectfully.

Back at The Falcon's Crest, the barley fields ripple with Ladakhi families singing ancient chants. Harmonious tones fill the air that resonate in my bones as if all is in order, inside and out. Good vibrations soothe my soul — light my imagination. The families chant all day as they harvest ripe barley on their knees with sharp, curved knives. The barley is gathered and stacked to dry for storage beneath house rafters in preparation for the harsh winter ahead. Between October and May, planes cannot land in Ladakh, and the dangerous mountain pass from Kashmir, 12,000 feet up to Ladakh, is closed. Ladakh is cut off from civilization.

Seven days into our three-week trip, I feel cut off from Bebe when she becomes madly besotted over a European mountain climber. Bebe declares she is leaving 'The Falcon's Crest' to spend time with him. Her hair is tossed back in seductive curls. I am in shock — afraid in massive mountains 6,000 miles from home.

I sit in my room, 'On Top of the World' yet 'Down in the Depths.' What am I going to do? Should I abandon the trip and fly home? Seeking guidance, I read the notes about Ladakh I had written before leaving home. My notes say that Ladakhis, like Tibetans, are honest, cheerful and non-judgmental. I must admit that Bebe is being honest when she declares her attraction to Mr. Mountain-man and her need to be with him. I am not cheerful and I am certainly judgmental.

Is a 'twist of fate' playing a wild card for me with Bebe?

3 MAGICAL CIRCLES

Seeking equilibrium from Bebe's discombobulating departure, I take a walk on a path up a hill near the Falcon's Crest. My heartbeats echo off the mountains, so still is the silence in the valley as I breathe three-dimensionally, likely taking in the cleanest air on earth. I inhale slowly through my nose and expand my whole torso. My torso contracts as I exhale the breath through my mouth. Three-dimensional circular breathing creates space for my organs to move and revitalizes my whole system with oxygen. I am ready for action.

On the path, several black-necked cranes peck. They are about five feet long and weigh around twelve pounds. The cranes' pretty pearl grey bodies are enhanced by black on the head, neck, legs, feet, and tail, with a dab of red above the eyes from Nature's awesome genetic palate. These rare birds live mainly on the Tibetan Plateau. Come spring, some nest in neighboring Ladakh. To find a mate, and to keep the flock together, they perform spectacular interactive dance rituals. China, India, and Bhutan protect them as an endangered species. Bhutan holds a yearly dance festival to honor them. In the Buddhist tradition, black-necked cranes are revered as a symbol of connectivity, longevity, and loyalty. An ancient Japanese myth states that cranes live for 1000 years and if 1000 origami cranes are made, a wish will be granted.

A 12-year-old Japanese girl, dying of leukemia after exposure to radiation from an atomic bomb, folded 644 paper cranes with a wish for peace before she died. Paper crane folding for good wishes is practiced in several countries, including Japan and America, whose war initiated this adoption of the crane.

Here in Ladakh, a 'real live' crane flaps its wings into an impressive eight-foot span. It takes off to circle above — probably to scout for intruders. I move away quietly, for the crane's peace of mind as well as my own. As I walk, the Tibetan chant springs to mind. "Om Mani Padme Hum." — I Salute the Jewel Within. To Swiss psychiatrist Carl Jung, the Jewel represents The Self — a self-balancing-self-regulating principle in the human mind. While homeostasis for the body is regulated by temperature, blood, nutrients, and oxygen, homeostasis for the mind, according to Jung's extensive research, is regulated by symbols in dreams, fantasies, and imaginings. Jung noted that a symbol for The Self may appear when a person is in crisis or in the process of transformation. Now I am in crisis — feeling abandoned by Bebe far from home. My self-balancing, self-preservation mechanism wisely brings to mind a 'salute' to center.

A golden spiral appears on the path ahead — a Stupa representing an image of the cosmos — a landmark on a pilgrim journey. Near the Stupa is a small Temple, snuggled into the hillside, its door marked with ancient Tibetan symbols. At the door stands a monk in a maroon robe. He greets me warmly, with hands in prayer. I return the gesture. He beckons me inside.

An aroma of old incense permeates the air in the assembly hall, dimly lit by yak butter candles. As my vision adjusts to the low light, I gasp at enormous mandalas painted in brilliant colors on the walls — circles containing images that represent the cosmos. In Sanskrit, mandala means 'Magical Circle', designed as an instrument for meditation to balance body and mind.

On one wall is painted a serene-faced monk plucking a three-stringed instrument, similar to a lute. The opposite wall reveals an enormous, intricately colored wheel of life — a sacred space to open up the unconscious and bring it to conscious light. As I gaze at these ancient paintings, my mind races with images that flash past too fast to hold. I let go and breathe.

Dazed by primordial mandalas, I step outside the temple to the brilliant circle of a blazing sun and reflect on a human egg as a perfect circle, as are lymphocyte cells which protect the body from infection. While pondering circles during this walk down an unfamiliar path filled with surprises, a tiny one-room cafe appears. I peek inside. A neatly raked dirt floor supports well-worn wooden tables and benches. Posters on the wall state 'Free Tibet'. A man of middle age, with a welcoming smile, stands at the counter. I smile back, sit on a bench and request a beer. A cool bottle of Indian Pale Ale soon appears. It tastes so good. A short and cheery twenty-something man wearing well-worn Western clothes sits nearby. He approaches and politely asks if he may visit with me.

"Certainly," I say, flashing back to Bebe's welcoming of Mr. Silkman to our table in Delhi just a few days before and giggle at the thought. He also giggles. Laughter is infectious in this region. His round open face and curious sparkling eyes are a delight. He says his name is Tsering and that he lives in the Tibetan Refugee Camp near here, with his wife, three children, and several other family members. Tsering tells me that he teaches English, geography, and history to Tibetan children in the refugee camp. His English is excellent.

I say, "My name is Ana. I am originally from England, now living in America where I have three children. Currently, I write and produce educational videos. Tibetan Buddhism intrigues me. Since Tibet's borders are now closed to foreigners, I have come to Ladakh."

Tsering smiles and asks if I would like to visit the refugee camp twenty minutes by bus from Leh. We agree to meet the next day. The sun sinks fast behind the mountains as I walk back to the Falcon's Crest. I rest in my room to reflect on this incredible day. Bebe takes a break from Mr. Mountain-man and stops by to make sure I am okay. The atmosphere is strained. I tell her about seeing black-necked cranes, ancient mandalas and meeting Tsering. She shows little interest and soon takes off. No matter. I am set to explore.

Early the next morning, I catch a rattly old bus and travel several miles on a pot-holed road to the camp. The bus lurches to a stop in the middle of a barren moonscape where Tsering waits to greet me.

"Jullah. Jullah" he says. I respond, "Jullah. Jullah." We walk to the camp, which accommodates 2,000 Tibetan refugees. Tsering says that the Indian government donated this land to Tibetans in exile. He points to a group of buildings made of red bricks that were created from the deep red soil around them. He says that like most Tibetans who live in the camp he was born here. His parents and grandparents escaped from China's brutal occupation of Tibet by trekking across the Himalayan mountains for weeks, finding safety in Ladakh.

In the center of the camp is a one-story, flat-roofed school building about half a block long, with many windows. Tsering says the windows bring in light and the flat roof conserves heat. Three and four generations live together in tiny houses around the school. Tibetans revere their elders and do not abandon them when they are old.

Few visitors come to this remote settlement nestled in a valley between massive snow-covered mountains. Tibetan children jump for joy, with cheers and laughter, to greet us. Families stand near their treasured abodes to watch. They smile and nod — hands in prayer. With scarcely any material goods, these Tibetans emanate pure joy. Their infectious laughter bounces off the mountains to echo ages past. My face aches from laughing. I feel as if I belong, like never before.

Tsering invites me to visit anytime. I do, five times during the two weeks left of my three-week trip, as if drawn by a magnet. On one visit, I ask Tsering about 'Buddha' nature and how it works in the camp to help people be happy and in tune with one another. He tells me that Buddha nature is the hidden essence of all people. Tibet's spiritual leader, The Dalai Lama, calls it the original clear light of the mind. Tsering says that after Buddha attained the enlightened state of being connected to all living things in the cosmos and being at peace with himself, without craving anything, his first teaching was the 'Four Noble Truths'.

"What are the 'Four Noble Truths'?" I ask.

Tsering says that the #1 truth concerns the suffering, anxiety, and dissatisfaction that comes with birth, growing old, illness and death. #2 refers to the origin of suffering as the stress of holding on to things that are constantly changing. #3 is the lack of satisfaction in things that never measure up to expectations, and #4 is the path that leads to ending suffering. I say, "So how does one find this path?" Tsering's eyes twinkle as he describes an eight-fold path that includes right view, intention, speech, action, livelihood, effort, mindfulness and concentration, and says that all elements on the path are linked together. Each helps to activate the other. Is this the true path to ending suffering and beginning enlightenment? I wonder how people pay attention to all elements at the same time. My view frequently changes with circumstance, and brings emotion that affects my intention, speech and action.

As for livelihood and effort, I do my best. My mind is often a scrambled egg. Currently, I have transitory control over it. I tell Tsering, with his curious Buddha nature, that I have much work to do if I am to develop my Buddha nature. He smiles.

As I enter the bus to return to the hotel, I hear Tsering calling "Tashi Delek" in Tibetan meaning 'Good Luck.'

Good luck I need when all is in motion, and I am ready for action with a clear light of mind through mindfulness, concentration, and meditation. This is a tall order for a woman who needs magical circles to keep her together.

4 IMPERMANENCE IN ACTION

On my next visit to the camp, I ask Tsering why China invaded Tibet, and closed Tibet's borders to foreigners? Tsering says that Tibet, independent for 2,000 years — with its own culture, language, and customs — was cleverly attacked by China in 1949 while the rest of the world was recovering from the second world war, too busy to hear Tibet's cries for help. He says that China captured Tibet for its strategic position in the heart of central Asia and for its vast animal, forest and mineral reserves. Minerals include gold, silver, copper and also uranium, of which China mines a lot in Tibet. Uranium becomes a prize commodity for China to sell to both sides in conflict — India and Pakistan, Iran and Iraq — and to countries that seek nuclear power such as Switzerland. Tsering says China closed Tibet's borders to foreigners so no-one could see what they were doing, raping Tibet of its resources and its people of their identity, livelihood, and life.

Tsering describes Tibetans as Buddhists who live close to nature with compassion and reverence for all living things. They practice non-violence and do not have weapons to defend themselves against China's military might. Chinese soldiers were ordered to destroy many monasteries — the Tibetans' main centers for art, meditation, advanced learning, philosophical debate, and worship.

When visiting the camp, Tsering told me many stories that stem from Tibetans who escaped over the mountains and from journalists who secretly crossed Tibet's borders to gather information and report facts to the West. Facts include horrendous violations of Tibetans' human rights and the destruction of Tibet's natural environment. Most disturbing for the whole world: China is said to be producing and testing nuclear bombs in Tibet — dumping their nuclear waste in Tibet and the waste from other countries as well, such as Switzerland. No one wants nuclear waste in their own back yard.

Back at the hotel, I am discombobulated by Tsering's stories. Now, 'On Top of the World', I am 'Down in the Depths' of my earliest memories in England of sirens roaring and bombs dropping, during WW2. I am sweating, and unable to catch my breath. The potential for 'a clear light of mind' is in shreds. Out of the blue I imagine producing a documentary video about the Chinese/Tibetan situation. This is not so far-fetched, since I am experienced in video production from having produced several commercial health-related programs.

Where images would come from, I do not know. I go back to the camp and tell Tsering my idea. While he sees my enthusiasm, Tsering also observes my sadness and asks, out of the blue, if I would like to visit the Dalai Lama's retreat home. I say, "Oh yes, if we will not disturb him." Tsering says that His Holiness is currently away in Dharamsala, where Tibet's government in exile resides, along with many Tibetan refugees.

We take off for the Dalai's retreat on a narrow, winding path, upon which we meet several goats being herded along. Pointing to the goats, Tsering says that is good meat going to market.

"But Buddhists don't eat meat," I responded to which Tsering declares that Tibetans eat meat. They just don't kill to eat.

"So, who does the killing?" I ask. Tsering says that the Muslims do it.

A judgment pops up immediately. Tibetans will eat meat but not kill to eat? Do I kill the meat I eat? So much for judgment. My thought melts away. My 'clear light of mind' is coming out to play.

As if reading my thoughts, Tsering tells me that while in New York, the Dalai Lama was served the finest organic brown rice and vegetables for dinner. At eleven pm, he ordered a New York steak. Apparently, The Dalai had been ill and his doctor advised him to eat red meat in order to recover. "Well fancy that," I exclaim as the path opens into a breathtaking valley, surrounded by massive mountains that sparkle a brilliant white against the bright blue sky.

In the center of the valley sits a flat-roofed dwelling with windows all around. It is about 800 square feet, made of mud bricks. Standing at the entrance is a tall, handsome Tibetan, wearing the maroon robe of a monk. His finely chiseled face emanates tranquility.

Tsering knows him. They chit-chat rapidly in Tibetan, and laugh frequently. The sentry smiles warmly at me as Tsering beckons me to follow him.

Upon entering this holy abode, Tsering prostrates himself several times before the Dalai Lama's altar and signals me to do the same. This is a challenge. To me, all people are equal, with none above the other, plus I am not very agile and my knees hurt. I do one prostration out of respect for the situation. As I stagger to my feet, Tsering gallantly offers me his hand.

I look around and feel the stillness fill the air. The main room is sparsely decorated with colorful Tibetan artifacts. I see the space around objects as art, not just the object itself. My perception is shifting when Tsering beckons me to follow him up stone steps to a flat roof where a 360-degree view takes my breath away. I walk slowly in circles around the edge of the roof and take 3-dimensional breaths in through my nose — out through my mouth.

Tsering stands by the railing watching me. The panorama is incredible. The energy coming in waves is palpable. Rainbow colors appear in and around everything — the valley, the mountains, and Tsering. Having experimented with psychedelic drugs during college days in the 1970s, I am familiar with altered mental states. However, here electromagnetic forces generate the same effect. This energy passes all tingle tests! I am speechless.

As Tsering and I walk back to the camp, I tell him that I saw 'space as art' in place of 'art in space' in the Dalai's retreat home and that rainbow colors appeared around everything, including him on the Dalai's roof. Smiling, Tsering says that the circular path I walked

17

spontaneously on the roof is the same path the Dalai Lama walks at 4 am for his first meditation of the day. Holy moly, no wonder I felt such strong energy while in this magical circle.

Years later, I wonder if this was an experience of 'The Golden Ratio' — a mathematical formula purported to operate as a universal law of divine proportions — a spiritual ideal striving for its fullest realization of beauty and completeness in the realms of art and nature. Is this the universal law that embraces magic in circles and spirals — the energy in the four noble truths and the eight-fold path that lead to immortality? All I know is that something happened to change my perception from seeing art in space to space as art and rainbow colors embracing objects.

"Tashi Delek," shouts Tsering as I board the bus. "Tashi Delek, dear Tsering," I return the call not knowing how much we would both soon be needing 'good luck'.

Back at the Falcon's Crest, dark clouds billow ominously over the mountains. The air becomes heavier — colder. The shift in barometric pressure hurts my joints. That night a relentless blizzard turns everywhere densely white. Stacks of barley, standing tall the day before, buckle beneath the weight of falling snow. Bebe stops by to say she is leaving for Kashmir in a taxi with Mr. Mountain-man. I splutter. "But we are due to fly out in two days. Why drive 160 miles on a treacherous mountain pass in this weather?" Bebe says sheepishly that I am welcome to join them. I shake my head. Being the third wheel does not appeal, nor does traveling in snowy conditions on a road notorious for accidents. Anyway, I must say goodbye to Tsering.

As heavy snow conditions prevail, Bebe takes off for her next adventure. Will I see her again? My children? My family? My friends? Will I die here? What hand will fate play with this wild card? Nature can be cruel for the people who live here. I recall the Ladakhi families chanting merrily when they cut and stacked the barley — their staple food for the whole year, ruined. I weep. This 'impermanence in action' is not funny. Bebe's departure has left me scared and alone 'on top of the world', but not 'down in the depths'. I am too anxious to be depressed. I have to see Tsering again. Now, with passionate intent revving for action about producing a documentary on the Chinese/Tibetan situation, I need more information.

I wrap warmly and walk to town in the snowy footprints of the local folk. All busses in and out of Leh are canceled. Determined to reach Tsering, I thumb a ride on a truck that appears moderately safe, with a beaming driver who welcomes company and hopefully a tip. He is a Hindu man, with a small replica of Shiva dangling from the rearview mirror. In Hindu mythology, Shiva is the all-encompassing auspicious one — a transformer — a destroyer — a cosmic dancer. I sit up front with the chatty driver, whose Indian accent I do not understand. I watch the shimmering silver Shiva wave arms and legs in a wild cosmic dance as we weave our way on a deeply rutted, bone-shaking, snow-impacted road to the Tibetan refugee camp, for what I know will be the last time.

Upon arrival at the camp, I am horrified to see that the school building and several houses are partly collapsed under the weight of deep snow on the roof. Camp members stand in huddles. Tsering sees me and waves. Our meeting feels more intense than before.

"I am so relieved to see you are safe," I say, "and so sad to see this devastation. Are you and your family okay?" Tsering says that they are all okay and urgently beckons me to follow him. We walk past several damaged houses to Tsering's abode. I gasp. His mud-brick home has completely collapsed from the burden of snow, and the old tin roof is a mangled mess.

"What will you do?" I ask. Tsering states that he will eventually re-build. Meanwhile, he and his 12 family members from four generations will live in the large tent that takes up every inch of the tiny backyard.

"But winter is coming." I gulp. Tsering says he knows it will be hard: however, Tibetans endure far worse in Tibet under Chinese occupation.

I ask, "Why are you so cheerful in such a catastrophe?"

Tsering smiles saying it is Karma to pay off an old debt. It is tempting to debate Karma in relationship to chance and Nature but not the right time to discuss such philosophical matters.

19

Tsering crawls on his hands and knees through rubble beneath the collapsed roof to the wreckage of his wire-framed bed. He lifts the shattered frame with one hand and precariously reaches under it with the other hand to drag out a square metal case — two feet long, two feet wide and a foot deep. What could possibly be in this box that Tsering risks his life to retrieve? Tsering slithers backward dragging the box. He reverently unclips the clasps and lifts the lid to reveal its only contents — a cream colored, embroidered wool shawl, and two booklets whose 60 or so pages turn out to be packed with information concerning the Chinese/Tibetan situation from a journalist and two M.D.'s who in the 1980's, were furtively in Tibet. Tsering places all content from the box in my arms. I put the shawl around my freezing neck and shoulders, and hold the booklets to my heart.

Tsering's wife appears. She greets me quietly, with hands in prayer, and beckons us past their devastated home to a small open-sided structure whose roof still stands. It is a tiny restaurant, run by Tsering's family to serve the community. This lovely lady, so gentle in manner, offers us a cup of tea. Thankfully it is not the Yak butter-salty variety that is so ghastly, to me. This black Indian tea, sweetened with condensed milk, is just like what I used to drink back home in England, especially during and after the war.

While Tsering and I sit on a bench sipping the delicious tea I thank him for the lovely shawl and ask him about the booklets. He says, with passion, that they are reports about China's invasion of Tibet, to help me write the script. I look at the documents.

One report is called, 'The Suppression of a People: Accounts of Torture and Imprisonment in Tibet' by John Ackerly and Blake Kerr, M.D., Physicians for Human Rights. Tsering states that, in 1987, these doctors went to Tibet for ten weeks and witnessed the deaths of many unarmed Tibetans.

The other report is called, 'Tibet Today: Current Conditions and Prospects' by John F. Avedon. Tsering says that Avedon is a Newsweek foreign correspondent who secretly crossed Tibet's borders several times to take pictures, collect testimonies and report back to America.

These documents appear essential to the work ahead.

With the warm shawl around me and the documents in one hand, with such sweet sorrow, Tsering and I hug farewell. Goodbye, dear Tsering. Goodbye.

I am fast asleep in my room, early the next morning when a loud knock on the door awakens me. It is a hotel guest saying that if I want to leave Ladakh I must go to the airport now. Only one plane is flying out, possibly the last one before Ladakh is cut from civilization until spring. I throw on more clothes, slam all else into my backpack and scurry out the door. This early winter storm is setting in.

With a heavy heart, I leave Ladakh — an amazing place of ancient Buddhism, nestled in the Himalayan Mountains. As I walk up the plane's slippery steps, I wonder whether the program I envisioned, 'Tibet: A Seed for Transformation. The Chinese/Tibetan Situation', will come to fruition or become a case of 'impermanence' in action'?

5 THE SPACE BETWEEN

Our plane plows blindly through dense clouds. No radar beams guide it between mountain peaks on the turbulent one-hour flight from the top of the world in Ladakh to its seemingly bottom in Kashmir. Through the Veil of Kashmir — named a veil for the mist that rises from Dahl Lake — the plane lands safely in Srinagar, where the tension between Hindus and Muslims is palpable — a far cry from the harmonious vibrations in Ladakh.

Why is there such agitation in Kashmir — a jewel in the heart of central Asia with majestic mountains, fertile valleys, lakes, and rivers in a mostly mild climate?

I recall from history that when Britain ruled India, between 1848 and 1947, Kashmir was a favorite place for the English elite to escape India's summer heat. To stop Hindus and Muslims fighting over territory and religious beliefs, Britain pressured India to split itself in two — an India primarily for Hindus and a Pakistan predominantly for Muslims. On the line of the split was the prize of Kashmir. In October, 1947, a Maharaja gave the State of Jammu and Kashmir to the union of India. This was done much to the chagrin of Kashmir's Muslim majority, who were not given a voice.

Now, in Kashmir, decades after independence, Hindus and Muslims still fight over who owns Kashmir. Gandhi did not think that splitting India was a good idea. He had worked diligently to harmonize his country and make India independent again. As was later emphasized during my training as a mediator, all parties must be at the table and be equally heard by an impartial mediator for a durable agreement to be reached. It is no wonder that this issue still remains unresolved.

I leave the tension downtown to enter a majestic hotel on Dal Lake, where Bebe and I have arranged to meet. The off-season price is reasonable in this luxurious colonial-style mansion, painted bright white with gold trim. Peacocks proudly parade about the manicured grounds — poles apart from hours before when I was 'on top of the world' while 'down in the depths' of a snowstorm. Now I sit warmed in the sun like royalty, with the aroma of jasmine from an immaculate garden. A breathtaking view of the lake and snow-capped mountains is ahead.

I am served high tea — British style — by a young male waiter. His starched white cotton attire is in stark contrast to the brown homespun Goncha worn by servers in Ladakh.

The shift in altitude and attitude send me early to my room, complete with its own bathroom and toilet paper, double bed, and clean cotton sheets. My thoughts turn to Bebe. Where is she? Is she okay? We are due to fly back to America the next day.

With sleep far away, the day's events led me to further ponder: how did Great Britain come to rule India? In 1612, a few wealthy British merchants and aristocrats in London formed the 'East India Trading Company' to develop international trade with India's valuable commodities — salt, silk, cotton, tea, opium and sodium nitrate, a primary ingredient in gunpowder (and later in rocket fuel). By using India's cheap and plentiful labor, profit from the trade of these goods was enormous. This profit helped to build the British Empire.

Britain accumulated sufficient wealth and power to account for half the world's trade through this company, which had its own army. The company imploded when Britain could not control the fight for supremacy between Hindus and Muslims. It disbanded in 1874 and turned its wealth over to Queen Victoria. While Gandhi and his fellow citizens won freedom for India from the British, Gandhi lost in his opposition to splitting India.

I wonder if implosion of an empire often occurs after explosion through exploitation? History reveals that over time power over others, not power with them, is a corrupt and unworkable hand to play.

Such intriguing thoughts are quickly diverted when a woebegone Bebe wanders in. Her Mr. Mountain-man is off on a flight back to Europe. While I feel relief that Bebe is safe after the hair-raising snow storm in Ladakh, my resentment toward her for leaving me continues, and she receives an icy reception. We hardly speak at the hotel.

I feel Bebe sobbing quietly beside me while on the plane back to America, I ask, "Are you okay?" She shakes her head and says she misses Mr. Mountain-man. She has fallen in love with him and may never see him again. Despite all, I feel sad for her. We primarily sit in silence for the long flight home, each wrapped in our own thoughts, emotions, and questions.

Back in America, Bebe and I keep in touch. She divorces her husband of some 20 years and moves into a cozy cabin in the woods. I return to the empty nest I had left. My three kids are already on their own. To fill the void, I work in earnest on the Chinese/Tibetan documentary springing from the conversations with Tsering, including the reports he gave me. Current information from Asia Watch and Amnesty International about Tibet is also included.

During this time of gathering information, I hear about a woman in my home town who has recently returned from traveling for three months in rural Tibet with a man she met along the way. Behind closed borders in occupied Tibet, these daring voyagers furtively moved around the countryside to shoot exceptional color pictures of the people and the landscape. Upon hearing of my project from a mutual friend, this woman kindly gives me permission to transfer some of her color slides to video for use in the documentary. These incredible images become the backbone of the project.

As if by magic, another friend who works with Amnesty International phones to say that a Tibetan man and woman will be in town this evening. Perhaps I would like to meet them. "Yes," I say, "indeed I would." These Tibetans agree to a video-recorded interview with me for the documentary. The woman, Kunsang King

— born in India — lives in Seattle, where she is an activist for the Tibetan cause. She shares information about the horrendous violation of women's human rights in Tibet. Nuns tortured and sent to hard labor camps. Women raped by Chinese men and forced to marry them, or be killed. Tibetan children taken from their parents to China for indoctrination into Chinese ways.

The man, called Llasang Tsering, was born in Tibet but lives in India where he is president of the Tibetan Youth Congress — Tibet's primary political party. Llasang, a man well-educated, in part at Harvard — is returning to India after attending talks with officials in Switzerland, whose squeaky-clean reputation holds a dirty secret about buying uranium from China that comes from Tibet with the agreement that China take back the nuclear waste from that uranium — likely going back to Tibet. Llasang also speaks of China's furtive nuclear activities in Tibet — the production and testing of nuclear bombs under a mountain in the region called Amdo, and the dumping of nuclear waste on the Tibetan Plateau. He relays that China has built the world's largest prison in a remote region, one that is capable of holding up to ten million prisoners, and that many Tibetans who demonstrated against China's occupation are there.

What these Tibetans, Kunsang, and Llasang, share in the videoed interviews becomes invaluable to the documentary. The timely occurrence of their passing through Olympia during the final information gathering stage in the project is again pure synchronicity.

At this stage of gathering a lot of audio and video — text and images — I conclude that to authenticate the program, I need Tibetan music and live footage of the Dalai Lama. This means one thing — go back to India. However, in addition to the Tibet project, I am now working full time as a visiting faculty member, teaching Jungian Psychology and Creative Therapies at the Evergreen State College, an experimental school in Olympia, Washington — where 12 years before I had been a student studying the same topics. Can I dash back to India over spring break? By taking a couple of days at the end of winter and the beginning of spring quarter, covered by fellow faculty, I carve out fourteen days, including travel.

Despite the antics in our previous trip together, I suggest Bebe join me on this wild adventure to shoot footage of the Dalai Lama — not knowing where he will be — in Ladakh, in Dharmsala, or if in India at all, and no way to find out beforehand.

Upon arriving in Delhi, Bebe and I catch a plane to Srinagar — hoping to fly up to Ladakh, where we imagine the Dalai Lama might be in his retreat home. Seeing Tsering again would also be incredible. However, we soon discover that Ladakh is still in the iron grip of the hard winter we had left a few months before, with no air or land transportation able to move. Meanwhile, we need a place to stay overnight in Srinagar, and find a two-bedroom houseboat on beautiful Dahl Lake that sounds reasonable. Such houseboats were originally built as floating palaces for wealthy Brits to retreat from India's blazing summer heat.

My fantasy of experiencing British history in a floating palace, be it now, in reality, a cold and battered one, takes a frightening turn when gunshots — likely between Hindus and Muslims — awaken me as they echo across the lake. This deranged political situation turns more sinister when a large, smelly, and hairy man slithers into my bed and tries to grope me. My screams mingle with the gunshots over an otherwise tranquil lake. This repugnant man leaps from my bed so fast a bullet would have missed him, even if I had one.

Bebe did not encounter a night-time invasion. She appears to slide through life unscathed. I am shaken.

With the terror of the night behind me, Bebe and I board a tattered 16-seat plane headed for Simla — a former British hill station in N. India, en route to catch a bus to Dharamsala — where we hope the Dalai Lama will be. Skeptical of a safe arrival in this contraption, I walk the plank regardless in my dance with fate. On this occasion, my skepticism reaches an elevated position while passing through the infamous Himalayan mountain chain. We hit an ice storm. I see through splattered windows the plane's wings tip scarily close to the mountain's edge as we toss and tilt in the tempest.

Fear overrides reason. Internal pressure mounts. I throw up in the bag provided. Several other passengers do the same. Across from me sits Bebe, unperturbed. Later, I ask her how she did this. Bebe said that she left her body and went back home to the comfort and safety of her cabin in the woods. Impressed, I vow to remember this technique if ever in danger again.

Over an inaudible intercom, the pilot tells us to hang on tightly, as we are about to make an emergency landing. I throw up again. The plane suddenly descends in a swiveling, swerving mass of metal to a wild slide on a snow-packed runway between mountain peaks. As the plane skids to an impressive halt, a collective cheer erupts from us passengers for the pilot who so skillfully brings us to safety.

Bebe and I stagger down the plane's slippery steps, dragging our backpacks through an ice squall into a desolate open space. The pilot ushers us to a barren building — not like any airport. He says that taxis will come to take us on the two-hour ride to Simla, for which we must pay. A mystery man who sat behind me on the plane asks if we would like to share a cab. He is tall and oddly handsome, with dark hair cut smartly short that sports tiny bleached-blond streaks. We agree to share a ride.

A turban-clad Sikh arrives in a taxi and beckons us to get in. Bebe sits in front; I sit in back with the mystery man. He tells us he is a doctor from Finland on his way to Calcutta, via Simla, to work with Mother Teresa. He says we are lucky to be alive. Apparently, the pilot told him that the plane hit an ice storm, with no deicers for its two propeller engines that would have seized up had he continued. Hence, the emergency landing. The doctor also says we landed at a secret Russian airfield hidden in the mountains of India where, in case of war, planes from Russia could land and take off to reach China. Holy moly! An international intrigue to boot!

The doctor recommends a hotel on top of the central hill in Simla that is within our modest means. Bebe and I share a room with single beds. The view is incredible. We see tiny villages far across the fields below. I walk down the hill, where its three tiers define people from different class systems. The upper class lives at the top. The middle class lives in the middle, while the lepers and beggars live in squalor at the bottom. I feel sad knowing that my country of origin took wealth from India and left this horror in its wake.

The next day, Bebe and I leave Simla on a bus for Dharamsala. The bus driver, mad as a March hare, races around the Himalayas carrying his 30 passengers crunched together on hard, wooden seats for a 12-hour journey on a roughly hewn road narrower than the bus itself. Wheels on one side of the bus occasionally slip precariously over the edge of a 3,000-foot drop below while opposite wheels sporadically bounce off the side of the mountain. The wild zig-zag ride makes some passengers ill. Not me. I learn quickly from Bebe to leave my body for a tranquil place. I imagine sitting in the sun near the gentle lapping of sea water in Olympia, Washington.

Meanwhile, a centrifugal force keeps the bus on the road and us on high alert for unpredictable ejections from our seats — only to end up in a different seat — which is unsettling, to say the least. We hurtle past tiny villages, like a bat from beyond, sometimes clinging by a thread to the mountainside. People, chickens, goats, and thin scabby dogs scatter wildly when they hear the raucous horn a blare by the driver whose breakneck velocity remains as constant as the tenacious drug he may be on. A fellow passenger tells us at the end of the journey that bus drivers on this route usually take speed and make bets on who can drive the fastest.

Bruised, battered and bewildered, Bebe and I arrive in Dharamsala at 8 pm. We are fortunate to find a room to rent in a small hotel run by a Tibetan family. It is too late for dinner. Before collapsing on the bed, hungry and weary, I ask the owner if the Dalai Lama is in town. If so, where may we see him?

BINGO! The Dalai is here. Deep relief. To see him, we must go to the monastery at 8 am and wait near the door for him to appear after he has performed the Buddhist initiation rites for Westerners.

I imagine Tsering saying, "Tashi Delek" for good luck. Lying on the bed exhausted, I feel giddy. Tomorrow I will see the Dalai.

Giddy is good. Good night.

6 NOTHING IS PERMANENT

The penetrating ring from my alarm clock at 7 am catapults me from dreaming into jeans, shirt, and sandals. Bebe sleeps on. I sling the movie camera over my shoulder and head out the door. No time to eat as I pass the Tibetan kitchen — its sweet aroma of baking barley bread floating gently in the cool morning air.

I walk for about five minutes on a narrow unpaved road to the monastery. Upon arrival, all is quiet, with few people to be seen. I look for a good spot from which to film the Dalai Lama when he comes through the massive, monastery doors. A medium-sized tree in winter-mode looks easy to climb. I scamper up it with my camera and perch 15 feet up for a perfect view. It is past 8 am — the time the hotel keepers said the Dalai will appear. With my camera ready for action, I wait and wait. Nothing is happening. I ask a man below if the Dalai is coming. He says that the Buddhist initiation rites begin at 8 am and take four hours to complete. The Dalai Lama will appear at noon.

Oh no — four hours up a tree. How will I pee?

Braced between branches, I look for distraction and see Tibetans, Indians, and a few Westerners gathering below. Some Tibetans wear traditional clothes to see His Holiness when he comes to town. I notice a Tibetan woman with 108 braids in her hair to remind her of her mantras. An older woman, with long gray braids wrapped in a figure of eight at the nape of her neck, thumbs methodically through

29

her prayer beads. Prayer beads tally how many prayers are recited.

An Indian man in a Nepali hat speaks with two Tibetan Rinpoches in long saffron robes standing by the temple doors. A Rinpoche is an 'enlightened' Lama who teaches the Dharma — meaning cosmic law and order. These men laugh together. Hours pass. While scanning the scene for something interesting, a tall and extremely handsome Tibetan man with a finely chiseled face and perfect teeth appears in the lens of my camera. He glances up at me, perched in the tree, and smiles. I nearly fall from my roost in a swoon of ecstasy at the pure beauty of his being. "The Dalai is coming. The Dalai is coming," calls Bebe from below. She arrives just in time to abruptly eject me from my fantasy. I aim the camera at the monastery doors.

The doors are opened by two Rinpoches in the golden robes. The Dalai appears. I maneuver a 180-degree turn — holding the camera steady as His Holiness walks slowly beneath my roost on a path lined three-deep with devotees. I shoot between gaps in the crowd. His maroon robe cannot be missed. He smiles and waves to all. Tinted glasses protect his eyes from an unblinking sun at high noon. He passes by and is gone. That's that. I have footage of the Dalai. We can leave now. But wait a minute — I would love an interview with him before I go. The next day I find the Dalai Lama's residence and ask the Tibetan gatekeeper if I may meet with His Holiness for a documentary about the Chinese/Tibetan situation. The gatekeeper tells me to come back at the same time the following day and he will have an answer.

Excited beyond measure, I go to the head office of Tibet's government in exile, where I meet the chief Tibetan human rights officer, and ask if he has information, images, and music that I may use for the documentary. He does and he agrees to share. We sit and chat in a sparsely furnished room that carries a whiff of Tibetan dumplings from the restaurant kitchen next door. He tells me about Tibetan refugees — men, women, and children who traversed the treacherous mountain pass across the Himalayas to his office for safety here in Dharamsala. These Tibetans brought first-hand accounts of the horror in their homeland under Chinese occupation. I am shown photos of the streets in Lhasa, Tibet's capital, where injured monks are running from the brutal attacks of Chinese soldiers. Shops are set on fire.

In addition to images, the human rights officer brings tapes and a cassette player. I hear a cry from the top of the world when a high-pitched female voice sings a lament in Tibetan. It fuels my imagination. Then I listen to the Dalai Lama chanting with his monks in Tibetan--a requiem from ancient Tibet. The tones resonate in my bones. Following this, I hear a speech in Tibetan given by the Dalai Lama about the Chinese government's unwillingness to discuss the care of Tibetans living in Tibet. I request a translation to English of this passionate soliloquy. How perfectly it fits the program. Permission is granted for use in the documentary of images, singing, chanting and The Dalai Lama's speech. The program is taking shape like a giant jigsaw puzzle.

Will the Dalai Lama do an interview with me? The next day I tremble with anticipation as I walk to the Dalai's home for the answer. The gatekeeper I saw the day before beckons me closer. He says that the Dalai Lama will meet with me at 2 p.m. in 3 days. My heart skips a beat. On that day, Bebe and I are due to fly back to America from Delhi. It is a 10-hour taxi ride from Dharamsala to Delhi airport. With no travel agent in town poor telephone communication and no computer connections in 1989 — changing flights in Dharamsala for America would be impossible. I am under contract to teach at the Evergreen State college the day I return, with no way to re-negotiate on short notice. I tell my dilemma to the Dalai's courier and plead for a way to meet His Holiness before I must leave. The courier walks back to the Dalai's abode and returns saying he is sorry — no other time is available. I thank him and walk away, deeply disappointed.

To pass the time, I walk about the small town of Dharamsala and shoot footage of village life. I spin the prayer wheels around the temple chanting, 'Om Mani Padme Hum', 'I Salute the Jewel Within,' to re-balance my disappointment. Despite the highlight plucked from my hand by time and commitment, I see all is not lost. The treasures given me are golden. I am thankful.

It is time to find a taxi to take Bebe and me on the ten-hour journey back to Delhi.

"Know anyone going to Delhi by taxi on Monday?" I politely ask a Rinpoche sipping tea in a cafe on the main street. He replies, "I am going that way to catch a plane back to Europe along with two other Rinpoches. There is room for all of us." Yes indeed, it could be an interesting journey with three holy men. Bebe and I climb into the front seat of a battered old taxi with a doddery looking driver. The three Rinpoches nestle together in the back seat. The car lurches and splutters as we take off on a gravel road with two narrow lanes — sparse margins on either side and many potholes. We ride for an hour or so, with little said, when a back tire bursts. The driver carefully maneuvers his beastie to the meager margin. Bebe and I pile out, followed by the Rinpoches. While the tire is changed, we all take a pee on the side of the road.

We are riding for another hour or so when the other back tire bursts. The driver maneuvers his jalopy to a safe stopping point. My anxiety level is rapidly rising. After sacrificing meeting the Dalai Lama, we may miss the plane and then what? I would be ticked off beyond measure. The driver has two spare tires, so all is well. We are soon back on the road.

Within 50 miles of Delhi, my heart almost stops beating when a front tire bursts, sending the taxi wobbling precariously across both lanes of the road. Rattly trucks and cars coming in the opposite direction swerve about and honk their horns. The driver of a donkey and cart moves aside as quickly as can be in the nick of time as we slide by, out of control. We come to a stop, facing a field. My heart is now racing as I step out of the car. This is it. We are stuck in a desolate place with no more spare tires. What now?

I am near hysteria while Bebe laughs with the Rinpoches in the field. My calm Buddha nature is far from this reality. I am very hungry. All the food we brought for the journey is gone, and there isn't a place to eat on this stretch of desolation. I am pacing frantically when another taxi driver pulls up alongside. Speaking Hindi, he asks our driver if he needs help. Soon this 'good samaritan' leaves with the best of the three flat tires, and returns in an hour with it miraculously repaired. In deep appreciation, we pile back into our taxi.

With little time left to catch the plane, I turn to the three enlightened ones sitting blissfully in the back seat and ask, "Why do the tires keep bursting?" The holy man in the middle smiles and says, "perhaps you should not leave India."

We arrive at the airport gate — the last passengers to board — and settle into our seats for the long flight home.

7 MUCH IN MOTION

After 30 hours of traveling back to Washington State, I arrive in the nick of time at The Evergreen State College to seminar with 25 students in the initial classes of the coordinated studies program, called 'Human Health and Behavior'. The program combines psychology, sociology, and human biology, involving four faculty members with 80+ students. In psychology, a key section explored Carl Jung's 'Structure and Dynamics of the Psyche'. Suggested reading: 'Man and His Symbols', by Jung and associates. This book would not have been written but for a dream Jung had the year before he died, in which he dreamed he spoke to a large group of people about his work and they understood every word he said. Until this dream, Jung had maintained that his work was too complex for the average person to comprehend. He followed this dream, and with the help of colleagues, spent the last year of his life devoted to creating 'Man and His Symbols' — a comprehensive book about his key concepts, with images to support the text. Jung died within 10 days of its completion.

Now, back at the college where I had studied Jungian Psychology and Creative Therapies for a B. A. degree, the students and I explore Jung's concepts in relation to dreams and imaginings in writing, art, and movement. Concepts include: The Personal Unconscious, where everything is stored that affects us personally. Complexes — psychological wounds that disrupt consciousness. The Collective Unconscious where everything is recorded that affects humanity, in the form of archetypal images. The Shadow — the part of ourselves we don't like and project onto others, and Synchronicity — when two meaningful events happen simultaneously.

For example — When Tsering told me about Mao Tse Tsung's merciless take-over of Tibet, my 'Personal Unconscious' recalled childhood experiences during WWII, when Hitler's 'will to power' sent bomber planes to attack England. My earliest memories include warning sirens roaring and the family huddle under the stairs for meager protection. This memory activated a primary 'Complex' — a psychological wound — that further spurred me into producing the documentary about Mao Tse Tung's 'will to power' which forged the Chinese/Tibetan situation. My 'Collective Unconscious' surfaced when I saw the huge Mandalas in a temple on the path to meet Tsering. Jung refers to Mandalas as symbols for 'The Self' — a self-balancing process in the human mind that works toward wholeness. Jung states that a symbol of the 'The Self' usually appears when a person is in crisis. I was indeed in crisis — abandoned far from home — when the Mandala appeared in the temple on the way, not yet known, to meet Tsering. Meditating on the Mandalas mysteriously calmed my mind. 'The Shadow' — the part of myself I don't like — was revealed in my anger toward Bebe. Upon reflection, I realized that at times, I too have been unconscious of how my actions affect others. 'Synchronicity' — when two meaningful events occur simultaneously. This concept appeared on several occasions during the adventure, as if all were in divine order. For example, meeting Tsering during a crisis. He taught me about Buddhism and informed me of the Chinese/Tibetan situation. Being offered superb photos recently taken in Tibet, and audio recordings of previously unheard chanting by The Dalai Lama and his monks. Then, the two Tibetan activists appeared who, for one night, were speaking in town while I was attempting to pull the program together with insufficient information, and they agreed to a videotaped interview that became essential to the program. None of this would have happened had Bebe and I remained together. None would have happened had Synchronicity not come out to play. None would have happened if I had not followed the path that appeared, while not knowing where the path would lead.

Now, at this innovative college that I love, the excitement generated

35

by the students as we explore Jung's concepts in relationship to life experiences largely relieves the disappointment I feel in not meeting the Dalai Lama in person.

When this teaching quarter is over, I dive into the information gathered about the Chinese/Tibetan situation. I sell some land to pay back my loans for travel and upcoming production costs. I live simply in a cabin in the woods. I haul water for washing and drinking and collect wood for heating and cooking. Electrical wire runs from the old farmhouse nearby to operate a TV, a VCR and a light at night. As I sit on the floor near my old wood stove, my head is often a scrambled egg. My tiny cabin is covered with pieces of paper holding conversations with Tsering, and the two booklets he rescued from under his collapsed bed after the devastating snow storm, as well as photos from the local woman who secretly trekked for three months across Tibet. There are photos given to me by the Human Rights officer in Dharamsala along with the precious cassette tape recording of the Dalai Lama chanting and his passionate speech about what China was doing in Tibet. Included in this now large collection of data to sort through and make decisions about are recordings of Tibetan women singing — video interviews with two Tibetans who passed through Olympia for one night — 8 millimeter film footage shot of children playing in Ladakh and the Dalai Lama in India, and reports from Asia Watch and Amnesty International. Shuffled into all of this were many pieces of paper with ideas for combining images, music, and text.

This project was far more challenging and complicated than the four health-related videos I had previously produced.

I read the notes I took from meetings and conversations with Tsering and re-read the report by Newsweek foreign correspondent, John Avedon, in which he describes China's human rights violations of Tibetans — the destruction of Tibet's natural environment, and the secret nuclear activities China was conducting in Tibet that could affect us all. I recall Tsering telling me that Avedon submitted this report to the U.S. congress in 1988, requesting that America stop trading with China, due to China's human rights violations in Tibet and China's massive destruction of Tibet's natural environment. Avedon's report was ignored. Instead, that same year, Congress named China to "most favored nation" status, easing trade restrictions.

It took three weeks of 12-hour days to story-board the weaving of the narration, the images, and the music into a tapestry. When the script is complete, I leave my cabin in the woods and go to a local video studio to record the narration and place the images, interviews and music onto 3/4-inch video for editing later. Half-inch video copies, including timecode, are made so I can now review and notate all the material into the form of a documentary using the VCR in my cabin.

Again, I leave the warm solitude in my cabin to enter a cool high tech professional video editing studio. Bright lights flicker from several monitor screens in an otherwise dark room. The aroma of coffee fills the air. The editor and I work diligently for two weeks straight to create a precisely timed 29-minute documentary on a master tape, ready for reproduction. At that time, a minute was requested by TV stations for other announcements, hence 29 minutes exactly.

8 WHEN ALL IS SAID AND DONE

The documentary opens with the title appearing over images of the spectacular snowcapped Himalayan mountains, carved in jagged lines against a brilliant blue sky. Colorful prayer flags crisscross mountain passes. A woman with a clear, high pitched voice sings a lament in Tibetan that seems to vibrate through this massive, high landform.

Haunting chanting by The Dalai Lama and his monks, underlies images of Tibet's destruction and the horrors Tibetans face. The voice of Nawang, the Tibetan Human Rights officer in Dharmsala, speaks over images of shops set on fire by Chinese soldiers in Lhasa, Tibet's capital, while bloodied monks run for cover. The narration, supported by stunning still images of Tibetans, monasteries and life in rural Tibet, paint a picture of the Chinese/Tibetan situation. The Tibetans Llasang and Kunsang who passed through Olympia at a critical point in the production of the documentary tell stories from their experience and those of Tibetans who escaped from Tibet. Kunsang spoke about the suffering of women and children. Women forced to marry Chinese men. Children taken from their homes to China to be indoctrinated into Chinese ways. Llasang shared his deep concern over China's nuclear activities on top of the world and the effect it could have on the rest of the world. All the while, images of prayer flags flying high in Dharmsala and Ladakh relay in the wind to the world the Tibetan philosophy of compassion and karma.

The text includes the Dalai Lama's five-point peace plan that was given to me by The Tibetan Human Rights officer in Dharmsala. The Dalai has tried repeatedly to negotiate this plan with the Chinese government, to no avail. The plan consists of the following:

1. Transformation of the whole of Tibet into a zone of peace.

2. Abandonment of China's population transfer policy which threatens the very existence of the Tibetans as a people.

3. Respect for the Tibetan people's fundamental human rights and democratic freedoms.

4. Restoration and protection of Tibet's natural environment and the abandonment of China's use of Tibet for the production of nuclear weapons and dumping of nuclear waste.

5. Commencement of earnest negotiations on the future status of Tibet and of relations between Tibetans and Chinese Peoples.

China continues to ignore the Dalai Lama's peace plan.

The video ends with Tibetan children waving in the Refugee camp in Ladakh, and Tibetan children playing in the playground in India. An uplifting song sung by Tibetan women supports contact information of ways to help Tibetans, and then the credits rollover billowing clouds above the mountains.

Footnote: After decades of killing and subduing most Tibetans, some Chinese soldiers have been withdrawn, and parts of Tibet declared open to the public as tourist attractions, with revenue paid to China. Off limits to tourists, for obvious reasons, are remote regions where thousands of Tibetans are still held in prisons and forced into hard labor. Also off limits to tourists are locations where China's secret nuclear activities under a mountain in Tibet occur — where the production and testing of nuclear weapons take place. Accounts of these activities are revealed in the video interview with Llasang Tsering, head of Tibet's political party.

In addition to deep sorrow for the Tibetans who suffered, and still suffer, from the loss of life, land and culture, there is grave concern about China's secret nuclear testing and the dumping of nuclear waste in Tibet. By stealing Tibet from its people, China also now own the rights of the water for most of Asia that springs from the top of Mt Kailash in Tibet, and runs in rivers and rivulets to sustain millions of people downstream in Asia. What if this water were diverted, or contaminated? China is called upon to become transparent about its nuclear activities in Tibet.

In the summer of 1990, the documentary 'Tibet A Seed for Transformation: The Chinese/Tibetan Situation' was finally ready for television and distributed on VHS tape. This is before DVD's became mainstream. Pacific Mountain Television network in Colorado released the program via satellite to nine million high schoolers, with permission to download. It was aired nationally on local cable TV channels. Distributors include The Meridian Trust in London, Tibet House in New York and Jupiter Video Productions in Olympia, Washington.

The program is available to view on YouTube under the title, 'Tibet: A Seed for Transformation. The Chinese/Tibetan Situation.' The author reading the story, 'On Top of the World and Down in the Depths' and the written version are available for download at Audible.com.

Upon reflection this journey, with its many twists and turns, changed my life. I learned about Tibetan Buddhism, Tibetan culture and the beauty of the people. I heard about the rape of Tibet for the purpose of China's massive economic expansion and the toll it has taken on Tibet and Tibetans. I developed a formidable respect for Jung's concepts in light of the everyday patterns of living, especially for his concept of Synchronicity. When Bebe left me for Mr. Mountain-man, I met Tsering, who introduced me to the Chinese/Tibetan situation. This encounter encouraged me to pay close attention to synchronistic events in and around me and to follow my curiosity no matter how difficult the path may appear to be. Bebe's and my journey in Ladakh gave Bebe welcome relief from a crumbling marriage and the courage to move on. It gave me the dramatic change I needed from raising three children as a single mother, and a broader perspective on life. After this surprising adventure. I will never be the same again.

ABOUT THE AUTHOR

W.A. Schofield, known by her middle name Ana, was born in 1942 in Northern England and came to America in 1964, with her husband, where they had three children. In 1977, Ana received a B.A. degree, emphasizing Jungian Psychology and Creative Therapies, from The Evergreen State College in Olympia, Washington. From 1986 to today, Ana has focused on writing, narrating and producing two children's stories, five health related instructional videos, and two documentaries — *Tibet a Seed for Transformation: The Chinese/Tibetan Situation*, and *Peace Please: Children and War* concerning the psychology of war and its effect on children. *Peace Please* won the Best of the Northwest award in the professional documentary category from the National Association for Local cable programmers. Most programs were, and some still are distributed internationally. Her children's audio story, *Adventures with Merlott: Deva Dolphin* and instructional video, *Beyond Ergonomics: Stress and Injury Prevention for the Computer Generation*, are currently distributed through Createspace.